Dedication:

For Jesus, our Greatest Advocate and Warrior.

For everyone in the arena
fighting these battles,

For everyone who has stepped
out from exhaustion,
doubt, or a lack of faith,

Know that the enemies lies
are shattered at the
threshold of Grace.

When you are ready, the arena awaits you.

SHATTER THE STRONGHOLDS
Prayer Book and Journal
Volume 1

BY AMBER LYNN & JENNIFER TRACY

Copyright 2019 Jennifer Tracy-Inspire, LLC

All Rights Reserved

ISBN-13: 978-0-9993987-5-3
ISBN-10: 0-9993987-5-3

Chapters

Introduction

~ A Note From Amber ~

As you begin, I pray over you a spirit of healing and openness and against any spirit of fear or condemnation. I pray that you would ask Jesus to make His presence known to you as you walk through these chapters, strongholds, and scriptures.

The lyrics in my song 'Shatter the Strongholds' came out of a season when I realized I didn't want to do my life without Christ; in fact, I wanted him involved in all of it. A line in the bridge says, 'My greatest shortcoming, my biggest downfall, is when I try to do life, without you at all.' Declaring those words was a turning point for me. With a glimpse of His great grace in my view, I knew I wanted to surrender my heart, mind, intentions, actions, my everything over to Jesus. The overwhelming love that surrounded me when I surrendered my heart this way is hard to describe. One thing I can say for sure is that His love continues to show up in beautiful and life-changing ways daily.

So much joy—unfailing, unchanging joy—was added to my life when I found freedom in believing who Christ says I am. I found more clarity and closure in many areas of my life as my mom and I wrote these prayers and filled these chapters. The running joke has been 'that the whole writing process felt just like getting to hang out with Jesus and my mom.' Going deeper in each area revealed where I still had a struggle. This process was an example of the many times I have seen (and been thankful for) the refining fire Jesus offers. I've had to keep leaning in when I see how my heart, mind, or life does not align with what I see Christ calling me to. I haven't always been so sure of the truth

I shared above. I battled years of self-doubt, lies and allowed the world to determine and fluctuate my value. In God's grace, love, mercy, and kindness; and in His Word and His promises I have found my true foundation. Great peace has covered my life in believing these two truths: my humanness doesn't change my worth, and I am found whole and wholly loved in the unfailing goodness and love of God.

Before this stage of life that I'm in now was a long season of survival. I knew I was strong, resilient, and confident in myself. And those are all good things, right? They were until the battle was too hard, too long, and I ran out of resources. I had intentionally lived in isolation, as I believed that was the only way to keep myself safe. These choices kept me 'safe,' but only safe from having authentic relationships. I loved others but always kept a distance between them and my deepest pain and fears. The walls around me had been built up so high. I had faced so many rejections. I thought it would be better to be alone and never risk the pain of another person loving me and leaving me.

And honestly, survival is impressive. I have heard and witnessed so many stories of those who have endured and overcome great adversity. Whether they survived mental health challenges, physical trauma, or dealing with severe loss, I've seen many courageous people fight and win brutal battles by knowing how to survive. Amid my own story, I didn't realize that I fit into this category of survival. I was surviving and not REALLY living. Jesus said that He came to give us life and that His message was good news. To my dry, scared heart, I was so afraid to believe it. The year I met Jesus, I knew I was experiencing something new for the first time. I realized in the deepest parts of my soul just how much I needed this Jesus I had just met.

A season followed where I walked through my doubt to find what His place was in everything. During that time, I used to think I would arrive or even had arrived. Now I know that it will always be a journey on this side of heaven, and I will never stop being refined. I will always be grateful for those who linked arms with me and surrounded me with love, encouragement, and grace while I found my initial footing. Those who reflected the heart of Jesus as I needed to find my footing and foundation again and again.

I want to encourage you to seek out community; you were made to do life with others. The spurring on of one another in our pursuit of Jesus is something that will change your life. It has certainly changed mine. As you journey, know that I am for you. I am cheering you on as you fight for your life and then as you seek to have joy in your life, again or maybe for the first time.

I want you to know that I feel for you in your time of pain, that I care for you in your time of growth and transition, and that I am praying for your heart to align with Jesus. I want you to know that finding your life in Christ will bring you many blessings and a peace that surpasses all understanding. I'm praying that no matter what the days ahead have for you, that you will find yourself closer to Him there.

All my love and all His blessings,

Amber

I wanted to let the world know that I find my truth and value in being a daughter of the highest King and that my hope is found in Jesus. This marks the day my mature heart made its claim for Jesus. I trust that He knows me, and He loves me. I want to live my life for Him.

December 9th, 2018   **August 26th, 2018**

I took the left leg out of the river of doubt and re-committed my life to Jesus. I had already been baptized when I was young, but this day was symbolic of letting go of the stronghold of DOUBT that grappled at my soul.

~ A Note From Jennifer ~

As we begin this journey, I feel I must share some of my deepest pains and strongholds that I have worked to overcome in my life with you. Digging deep into our beliefs, the struggles that haunt us, and how different strongholds play out in our lives is no easy thing.

For many years I was stuck in the "Jesus where were you?" train of thought... That started when a 14-year-old boy stole my innocence as a 6-year-old little girl. After much therapy and intensely looking into God's word, I realized He was there with me... weeping... I wish I could tell you that being raped at 6 was the only trauma I've endured, but it's not. I buried a husband and a child at the age of 29. Three years later, I buried my mother. Five years after that, I survived traumatic brain surgery that left me with a titanium plate in my head and permanent nerve damage. Why do I share all of this with you? There is something about all of those things that I just listed that is very, very important to see. Those were all things that were out of my control. None of those things were my fault. I was a victim, yet I looked for what I could learn from those experiences and how to keep moving. Still, there was a lot of pain, and with that, a lot of strongholds were attached to the pain. As a high-functioning, driven woman, I can't stand to lose - I hate feeling powerless. Focusing on what I could control was essential during my survival and recovery.

Through all those trials and pain, I never lost faith. Not even after the death of my husband and daughter. BUT, after my brain surgery in 2012, after so much trauma I was stuck. It felt like I had one foot in the river of doubt with an anchor on it and the other foot in the river of faith with an anchor on it, unable to let go of either. I've recently learned there is a word for this, Ambivalent (the holding on to two opposing emotions, refusing to let go of one or the other.) With one foot in the river of doubt and the other in the river of faith, I was stuck. I was doing life alone. I was beyond tired with minimal trust or confidence in the Creator of my soul. For the first time in my life, I found myself making poor choice after poor choice with no one to blame but myself. Then the shame came. Then guilt. Then remorse. Then more guilt and shame. At one point, I wasn't even sure if I was a Christian. I remember looking in the mirror and thinking, "I don't recognize YOU." You can ask my daughter, Amber. She was 16 at the time and still living at home. I had hit rock bottom. You may think being suicidal or even losing my loved ones was my all-time low, but the truth is it was in the pit of my own poor choices. It was then that I realized how truly hard it is to forgive yourself when you know that YOU alone are to blame for the life that is staring back at you in the mirror. The only relief I found was when I would listen to my Christian music and worship God, which I frequently did. I think listening to my Christian music was one thing that kept my right foot so anchored in the river of faith.

At the end of me, the only thing that soothed my soul was learning to soak in the truth that I could keep running to Jesus over and over in my shame. I could hear Him say, "She's mine; I know her story. Leave her alone." Can you imagine someone fighting for you in the midst of your foolishness and disgust? WAIT, did you catch that? Someone fighting for you in the midst of your disgust. When is the last time someone did that for you?

That's my Jesus. No condemnation, no finger-pointing, only the gracious nudge to let Him heal me. So often in the mess, we run. Why? THIS is what has inspired me to take on this series with Amber. Battling strongholds takes time and requires us to tap into multiple resources, but none of those will heal the soul like the grace and mercy of Jesus Christ.

As we take on this series, I want you to know that I've worked my way through many strongholds and mastered them. Others, though not where I want to be, I can still say I'm further along than I was. Again, I share this with you because I want you to know you are not entering into this arena alone.

Chances are, I've been where you are, and WE are not entering this arena alone. Jesus, our greatest advocate, is with us. Every day, before I step into the arena, I let my heart beat to this mantra and tune...

"Until the day I die, I will live, breath, and work to Shatter The Strongholds in my life. One by one, with the help of my Creator, I will do it without guilt, shame, fear, or regret! I will do it knowing my redemptive work has already been done; eternity is mine, forgiveness is mine, grace and mercy are mine to rest in... Thank you, Jesus, my loving Advocate, and Faithful Friend... As my daughter, Amber, so beautifully wrote, 'When I give in, when I fall on my face, I'm always mesmerized by the amount of your Grace, my greatest shortcoming my biggest downfall is when I try to do life without You at all.'"

Thank you, Jesus; truly, without you, I'm nothing at all...

How the song paved
the way for the series...

Amber's story

At the time I wrote Shatter, I had already written over 100 songs. Sharing a new song with my mom was very normal for the two of us; however, this time something was different. This was the first time my mom "could hear herself singing my lyrics". She told me she felt like I had written the song just for her heart and her story!

Working together has always come naturally to us. Creatively, we are almost always on the same page. We're known for finishing each-other's thoughts and even randomly singing the same lyrics out of nowhere. Shatter was special, though, because it was the first time we had ever collaborated this way.

Jennifer's story

I do not consider myself a songwriter. What I experienced when I read Shatter was a first. There was immediately this distinct melody playing in my head. This came at the end of a season when I was calling myself "a doubter for Jesus." I had been moved by the Holy Spirit to be baptized just 5 months prior. Getting baptized was symbolic of me letting go of my doubt. Amber's song was the healing salve that anointed my soul. It reminded my heart that he saw all of me and had never left me. All of this felt like a spiritual beckoning...

Amber & Jennifer

The writing and creation of Shatter wrecked our hearts in the best way possible. It started a new fire in us, stirring up a bigger, bolder pursuit of Jesus. An overflow of the song was this journal, and whatever is to come, an overflow of all that Jesus is doing in us. Every piece of our life is an overflow of Him.

The idea of strongholds did not die with the writing of Shatter - the song was actually the first spark! We haven't been able to let go of the idea that Jesus wants us to find freedom and break off strongholds. After the song was completed, we continued to wrestle. That's what brought about this series!

Shatter The Strongholds

I bow at your alter, I sit at your feet,
I look up, I beg you to see,
Past my decisions, Into my dreams

Lord I ask of thee, Come, Shatter the Strongholds In me

I give into flesh, I lose sight of the sea,
I'm Buried under nets, I'm dying to breathe
I know what you say is true, No matter where I run,
There you are too

I know who you are, God of your word,
Over my heart, You've placed a guard

My maker, Creator, Jesus, my savior Come, Shatter the Strongholds in me,
Come, Shatter the Strongholds in me

So selfish, So inwardly focused
I struggle, I stumble, I'm not who you call me to be

Jesus, come, Shatter the Strongholds In me

When I give in... When I fall on my face... I'm always mesmerized,
By the amount of your grace
My greatest shortcoming, My biggest downfall,
Is when I try to do life... Without you at all...

Jesus, come, Shatter the Strongholds In me,
Jesus, come, Shatter the Strongholds In me

Your love Never fails, Your love Never gives up,
Your love, Never grows weary

Come, Shatter the Strongholds in me

Jesus, Jesus, You gave up the breath in your body
The life in your bones, You were nailed to that cross,
So now you sit on the throne
The greatest gift, I can truly give,
The only gift at all Is my life

I ask for the courage, To deny anything that isn't, You my Jesus
I ask for the courage, To seek you as you would have me my Jesus

Jesus, come shatter the Strongholds in me
I pray over my life,
That I would live and die,
Singing of you, Jesus

Jesus, Jesus
I bow at your alter, I sit at your feet
My maker, Creator
Jesus, my savior
Jesus, come
Shatter the Strongholds In me

Before You Begin

We are expectant and excited for your journey through these 10 strongholds. Each chapter will have an array of formats to process through--hopefully something for everyone!

Each stronghold will include:

- a scripture
- an introduction
- a coloring page
- pages to journal on
- a few reflection questions
- an area to set your hearts' intention
- & a discussion of how Jesus can relate to our struggle

Let the coloring pages serve you whatever purpose you need. Whether that is to doodle while you pray, to decompress with God, or to spend some time reflecting—whatever your heart needs! Coloring is not everyone's forte, so feel free to skip on past the designs if that's you, but do take a moment to read the words atop each page. 'His Banner Over Me is Love' is a line from a song we recalled when writing these prayers. We felt Jesus was asking us to share this beautiful reminder and promise with you. Whether you're battling through one specific stronghold or if the weight feels more like you are only getting through another day, remember—HIS BANNER OVER YOU IS LOVE!

Invite Jesus into these places with you—the good, the bad, the ugly, the hard, and the joy! If any doubt ever creeps in regarding your worth or who Jesus says you are, join with us to whisper, shout or cry out, 'No, HIS BANNER OVER ME IS LOVE!'

Know that as you embark on addressing and challenging different strongholds in your life, big thoughts and feelings will come in waves. Be prepared that you may find yourself having new thoughts along this journey. Some of these may be lovely, and some may feel discouraging or uncomfortable. That is completely normal.

You can do two things with this series! First, you could just read the journal as is! However, if you want more, we've got it! If you are looking for more depth or continued conversation, there is a guided book series that will journey through each chapter. More information about this can be found on our website.

By definition, a stronghold is "a place that has been fortified so as to protect it against attack" or "a place where a particular cause or belief is strongly defended or upheld." It's something that is tightly knit together that bonds you. That's an amazing thing if you're being held tightly by, say, love? Or in compassion, understanding, or joy? But in the opposite case, it's a horrendous reality to be knit together by any notion that you are unworthy, undeserving, insufficient, that you could be too far gone or that you are not what the words of Christ say you are. As you process these areas of your life, we pray/hope that you find yourself more and more wrapped up in Jesus's truth and promises.

Take heart. Lean into the positive, stronghold truths that God says over you. This book contains 10 strongholds. Know that moving through even a single stronghold is taking a huge step closer to being free.

Rather than the well-known quote "Jesus loves me, this I know," we heard it said once "Jesus knows me, this I love." Have you ever thought about how entirely you are known by Jesus and how fully he loves you? That's a beautiful thing about this relationship that Jesus wants so desperately to have with you – that by him, you are completely known and entirely loved. Where else in life on earth can you experience that? The closest we can come to this is in our authentic, loving relationships. However, nothing could ever compare to the love of our Savior.

One of the best ways we know to ask you to approach this book is through an analogy shared in our first book, From The Deepest

Darkness To The Light of HOPE, in the chapter entitled, "When God Ran."

" Stop for one minute and think about your fingerprint. In all of creation, there is only one that matches yours. YOUR fingerprint is so unique it can be scanned and traced to you whether you are in Africa or Atlanta. When you stop to consider all of the life circumstances that have brought you to this moment, is it any wonder that you would have a personal unique relationship and set of beliefs about gods or God? Has it ever occurred to you that when you ask God for help he has to deal with you the same way you do? He has to help you with the physical, mental, emotional and spiritual parts of you! Take some time to look at your own life through this lens. "

Every one of our journeys is going to be as unique and different as our fingerprints are. It is with this grace-filled and loving mindset towards ourselves that we are asking you to begin.

We have both read through God's whole story, the Bible; however, we want to be clear that neither of us are theologians. We are two women who wake up in the morning excited to talk about the Jesus we know. It is our heart to share our thoughts about Him with you! It's been a passion and joy to study his word. Both of us own multiple translations and study bibles that we love reading from. We love seeking out stories of what God is doing and how He is moving in the lives of everyone we meet!

Our childhood stories look different. One of us grew up with a relationship with Jesus, and the other "met Jesus" at eighteen. However, we both had God's Word written on our hearts from a young age, and we couldn't be more grateful for that!

Both of us have gone through seasons of extreme doubt that led us to places where we felt like we couldn't trust or feel God. In 2018, we both recommitted our lives to Jesus and chose to be baptized again. Since then, we have seen God's Word re-activate in our lives in unique and personal ways. It's been a joy and a blessing to partner with God to write this journal for you.

Again, we are expectant and hopeful over your journey. We are so honored to share our hearts with you.

Amber and Jennifer

Shatter the Stronghold of

Control

I planted the seed, Apollos watered it, but God has been making it grow.
- 1 Corinthians 3:6

Prayer

Jesus, I know you are my one true advocate. You are always present and always working. I trust that you are in the arena, ready to fight with me as I battle this lie. Come, shatter the stronghold of control in me.

Thoughts we ponder...

HOW DID JESUS PROCESS CONTROL? HE CHOSE SURRENDER. WHAT COMES AFTER WE SAY 'THY WILL BE DONE?'

When we hear Jesus say, "yet not my will, but yours be done." (Matthew 26:39), we focus on his surrender and how he had to release control over to God in that choice. We want to look at the truth that while God is moving and doing his part, he is also requiring us to do ours. Jesus did not end up aligned in Gods Will without intention and action on His part. Jesus came to live out the perfect example of walking with God in faith. He wants us to remember we still have to do our part. In being faithful and obedient to God, action is required.

Let's Take This To Jesus ~

Jesus, encourage me to breathe and find rest in controlling only what is mine to control. I want to live in your will for my life. Please place peace in my spirit to know that you are not angry with me when I try to control what's out of my hands. Soften my heart towards the learning process of understanding the difference between where you call me to action and where you call me to surrender. I want your will to be done more than anything, Lord. Please give me ears to hear You and equip me in how to follow you.

REFLECTIONS FROM THE HEART

When looking at this stronghold...

What is Jesus revealing to you?

Does this perspective differ from what you thought before? If so, how?

What new thoughts are you having?

How can His unconditional love encourage you?

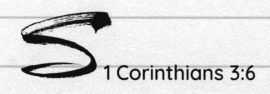
1 Corinthians 3:6

1 Corinthians 3:6

MY INTENTION

AWARENESS

What have I become aware of in this chapter?
What is something new I've learned?

BELIEF

What were my thoughts around this stronghold
before and after? Did I uncover any lies?

COMMITMENT

What truth will I move forward believing? Is there
something I want to stay committed to working on?

Intentions

1 Corinthians 3:6

1 Corinthians 3:6

His Banner Over Me is Love

Reflection

Shatter the Stronghold of

Insecurity

But God demonstrated his own love for us in this: While we were still sinners, Christ died for us.
- Romans 5:8

Prayer

Jesus, I know you are my one true advocate. You are always present and always working. I trust that you are in the arena, ready to fight with me as I battle this lie. Come, shatter the stronghold of insecurity in me.

Thoughts we ponder...

HOW DOES CHRIST OFFER US A STATE OF BEING EMOTIONALLY & SPIRITUALLY FREE FROM DANGER OR THREAT?

We must trade the security of this world and our own insecurity for the only true security: Jesus. Our hearts light up at this topic because this is the reason Jesus came down to earth. He came to show us that he knows what it's like to be separated from God. The longing that we know, he knows too. During his time here on earth, he broke tradition to seek the lost and reveal his true nature and heart. Jesus spoke to the woman at the well in John 4 about the living water that satisfies our thirst unlike anything else. We find his adamant love for us and this assurance of who we are only in knowing Jesus and being known by him. He wants your life to be full of joy, peace, and freedom.

Let's Take This To Jesus ~

Jesus, thank you for caring so much about my heart that you would come down and bear the pains of being human to show me your love, life, way, and truth. The more secure I am in you, the less insecure I am about myself. Understanding this in my soul strengthens my resolve to go out and be who you call me to be. Thank you for how much you love me. I want to live a life marked by your nature and goodness. Please give me the courage and equip me to hear your voice.

REFLECTIONS FROM THE HEART

When looking at this stronghold...

What is Jesus revealing to you?

Does this perspective differ from what you thought before? If so, how?

What new thoughts are you having?

How can His unconditional love encourage you?

Romans 5:8

Romans 5:8

MY INTENTION

AWARENESS

What have I become aware of in this chapter?
What is something new I've learned?

BELIEF

What were my thoughts around this stronghold
before and after? Did I uncover any lies?

COMMITMENT

What truth will I move forward believing? Is there
something I want to stay committed to working on?

Intentions

Romans 5:8

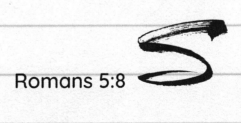

Romans 5:8

His Banner Over Me is Love

Reflection

Shatter the Stronghold of

Comparison

Let us run with perseverance the race marked out for us, fixing our eyes on Jesus
- Hebrews 12:1

Prayer

Jesus, I know you are my one true advocate. You are always present and always working. I trust that you are in the arena, ready to fight with me as I battle this lie. Come, shatter the stronghold of comparison in me.

Thoughts we ponder...

HOW CAN YOU FOLLOW JESUS' MODEL, AND RUN THE RACE SET BEFORE YOU, WITHOUT COMPARING OR COMPETING?

When we read Hebrews 12:1, it might be easy to think that Jesus would be more proud of us if we beat our component. However, the truth here is that we all have a race that is only ours to run. He wants us to give our best to the race that we are called to run. You running well has nothing to do with how the person next to you is running. Jesus wants them to win the race, too, their race. The solution here is not easy, but it is simple. We can become a better 'runner' by asking Jesus daily questions like this about your race: "Is this something you're calling me to?... Have you put this desire or passion on my heart?... How can I move in this situation in a way that brings you glory?... In what ways are you moving, Lord?" Suppose you can get in the habit of asking these kinds of questions and inviting Jesus in to your daily life and routine. In that case, I think you will be surprised by the clarity and peace he can add to your life.

Let's Take This To Jesus ~

Jesus, you have set before me a race to run, a life to live that is specifically and uniquely mine. Encourage me to step fully into who you call me to be and to the places you call me to go. Lord, please help me stay focused on my part in the story you have written. You know how difficult it is not to look around at what others are doing and accomplishing. When I listen to you, I hear that you say I am 'loved, significant, beautiful, unique,' Allow your powerful truth to change everything in me.

REFLECTIONS FROM THE HEART

When looking at this stronghold...

What is Jesus revealing to you?

Does this perspective differ from what you thought before? If so, how?

What new thoughts are you having?

How can His unconditional love encourage you?

Hebrews 12:1

Hebrews 12:1

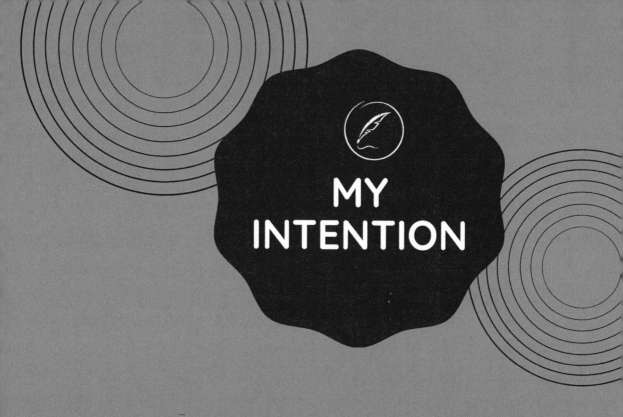

MY INTENTION

AWARENESS

What have I become aware of in this chapter?
What is something new I've learned?

BELIEF

What were my thoughts around this stronghold
before and after? Did I uncover any lies?

COMMITMENT

What truth will I move forward believing? Is there
something I want to stay committed to working on?

Intentions

 Hebrews 12:1

Hebrews 12:1

His Banner Over Me is Love

Reflection

Shatter the Stronghold of
Jealousy

A heart at peace gives life to the body, but envy rots the bones...
- Proverbs 14:30

Prayer

Jesus, I know you are my one true advocate. You are always present and always working. I trust that you are in the arena, ready to fight with me as I battle this lie. Come, shatter the stronghold of jealousy in me.

Thoughts we ponder...

IS JEALOUSY AN AWARENESS OF A DESIRE PLACED BY JESUS ON OUR HEARTS?

We've seen two kinds of jealousy that exist in our lives. One is a natural result of who God has called each of us to be and the lives he's called us to live. The other, however, is a result of sin in our lives—when we desire for things God would not have us want. In the New Testament, there are many stories of people who were jealous; Jesus' response varied depending on which type of jealousy sprung up in them. We need first to become aware of what type of jealousy is a part of our life. Identifying this will help us know how we ought to respond. Next, we need to invite Jesus and the Holy Spirit in to our thoughts and hearts to guide us to respond appropriately.

Let's Take This To Jesus ~

Jesus, as I pray, I bring my jealousy to you. I ask that you help me process how to respond to it. Please don't allow my feelings of jealousy to turn into an action that negatively affects how I process things. I pray for all bitter seeds of jealousy to be removed from my heart. I ask for the courage to always turn to you for the answer when I encounter the longings you have placed on my heart. I know that you want abundant life for me. Give me a heart that desires what you want so that I can think and act as you do.

REFLECTIONS FROM THE HEART

When looking at this stronghold...

What is Jesus revealing to you?

Does this perspective differ from what you thought before? If so, how?

What new thoughts are you having?

How can His unconditional love encourage you?

Proverbs 14:30

Proverbs 14:30

MY INTENTION

AWARENESS

What have I become aware of in this chapter?
What is something new I've learned?

BELIEF

What were my thoughts around this stronghold
before and after? Did I uncover any lies?

COMMITMENT

What truth will I move forward believing? Is there
something I want to stay committed to working on?

Intentions

Proverbs 14:30

Proverbs 14:30

His Banner Over Me is Love

Reflection

Shatter the Stronghold of

Abandonment

Lord, you have seen this; do not be silent. Do not be far from me...
- Psalm 35:22

Prayer

Jesus, I know you are my one true advocate. You are always present and always working. I trust that you are in the arena, ready to fight with me as I battle this lie. Come, shatter the stronghold of abandonment in me.

Thoughts we ponder...

DO YOU THINK THAT JESUS EVER FELT ABANDONED?

In Matthew 26, Jesus talks about a time before his death when he went to pray, and his disciples fell asleep. We can't fathom the depth of how immensely he must have felt abandoned. This was the time when he needed those closest to him the most. As the hour of his death approached, Jesus cried out to God, saying, "Why have you forsaken me?" (Matthew 27:46) Can you imagine the depth of abandonment that Jesus was experiencing? Reading through this account has helped us to trust that Jesus can relate to us. He knows emotional and physical pain, as all humans do.

Let's Take This To Jesus ~

Jesus, when the hour of your death was upon you, it was then that you knew the deepest feeling of abandonment when you were separated from the Father. Oh Jesus, help me to believe you when you say you will never leave or forsake me. When I cry, "Do not be far from me, Lord," help me to trust your nearness. Even when everything that surrounds me says I am abandoned, I will move forward believing what you say is true. You say you are near to the brokenhearted; I will trust this promise.

REFLECTIONS FROM THE HEART

When looking at this stronghold...

What is Jesus revealing to you?

Does this perspective differ from what you thought before? If so, how?

What new thoughts are you having?

How can His unconditional love encourage you?

Psalm:35:22

Psalm:35:22

MY INTENTION

AWARENESS

What have I become aware of in this chapter?
What is something new I've learned?

BELIEF

What were my thoughts around this stronghold
before and after? Did I uncover any lies?

COMMITMENT

What truth will I move forward believing? Is there
something I want to stay committed to working on?

Intentions

Psalm:35:22

Psalm:35:22

Reflection

Shatter the Stronghold of

People-Pleasing

Fearing people is a dangerous trap,
but trusting the Lord means safety.
- Proverbs 29:25

Prayer

Jesus, I know you are my one true advocate. You are always present and always working. I trust that you are in the arena, ready to fight with me as I battle this lie. Come, shatter the stronghold of people-pleasing in me.

Thoughts we ponder...

DO YOU THINK THAT JESUS HAD TO CHOOSE BETWEEN PLEASING PEOPLE OR PLEASING GOD?

In Luke 14, Jesus talks about when he met a man on the Sabbath who was suffering. It was against the cultural norm (and even law) to heal on the Sabbath because healing was considered labor. Jesus confronted the teachings of the time by asking, "Is it lawful to heal on the Sabbath, or not?" He went on to compare healing to saving your child or an animal that may have fallen into a well on the Sabbath. Jesus was implying, 'Would you leave your child in a well after they have fallen, because of the Sabbath? Today, this might seem like common sense for a doctor to still work on a Sunday or Sabbath day, but in those days this was not the case. Jesus was making a statement. He made it clear that he cared more about God's heart and priorities than that of man's-- even men with authority, since their belief and law following contradicted God's heart.

Let's Take This To Jesus ~

Jesus, you took this stand for what was right, knowing you may have had to suffer the consequences of breaking man's law to honor God. In your time on earth, you were tempted in all of the ways I am in my humanness. You came to be my example. Your life showed me perfectly how to walk out my faith in God. Please give me the strength to choose pleasing God over pleasing man, no matter the consequences.

REFLECTIONS FROM THE HEART

When looking at this stronghold...

What is Jesus revealing to you?

Does this perspective differ from what
you thought before? If so, how?

What new thoughts are you having?

How can His unconditional love encourage you?

Proverbs 29:25

Proverbs 29:25

MY INTENTION

AWARENESS

What have I become aware of in this chapter?
What is something new I've learned?

BELIEF

What were my thoughts around this stronghold
before and after? Did I uncover any lies?

COMMITMENT

What truth will I move forward believing? Is there
something I want to stay committed to working on?

Intentions

Proverbs 29:25

Proverbs 29:25

His Banner Over
Me is Love

Reflection

Shatter the Stronghold of
Self-Condemnation

*Therefore there is no condemnation
for those who are in Christ Jesus
- Romans 8:1*

Prayer

Jesus, I know you are my one true advocate. You are always present and always working. I trust that you are in the arena, ready to fight with me as I battle this lie. Come, shatter the stronghold of self-condemnation in me.

Thoughts we ponder...

AS A CHRISTIAN, WHY DO I STILL FEEL SO MUCH SHAME AND GUILT, IF CHRIST DIED TO TAKE ALL GUILT AND SHAME FOR ME?

In Romans 8:1, Paul writes, "Therefore there is no condemnation for those who are in Christ Jesus." If this is true, why do so many of us still walk around feeling guilt and shame? Why do we run away from God when we are struggling? Dear friend, it may be time that you realize that sometimes you are condemning yourself for what you have done. It is so important to evaluate where the shame and guilt are coming from. Yes, the enemy likes to remind us of our sins and struggles. The world is not always kind or helpful in our healing process, but take time today to evaluate if you are condemning yourself.

Let's Take This To Jesus ~

Jesus, please remind me any time that I feel guilt and shame, that you have already paid the price for all of my sins. Give me eyes to see that you approach me when I am struggling, with grace and mercy, and that your deepest desire is to see me move through my stronghold and be set free from it. Jesus, encourage me to come into your presence, and please bring me awareness when I am condemning myself. You want me to live a life free of lies and to walk in freedom. Please equip me for all that is to come. May I become who you have called me to be.

REFLECTIONS FROM THE HEART

When looking at this stronghold...

What is Jesus revealing to you?

Does this perspective differ from what you thought before? If so, how?

What new thoughts are you having?

How can His unconditional love encourage you?

Romans 8:1

Romans 8:1

MY INTENTION

AWARENESS

What have I become aware of in this chapter?
What is something new I've learned?

BELIEF

What were my thoughts around this stronghold
before and after? Did I uncover any lies?

COMMITMENT

What truth will I move forward believing? Is there
something I want to stay committed to working on?

Intentions

Romans 8:1

Romans 8:1

His Banner Over Me is Love

Reflection

Shatter the Stronghold of

Rebellion

The son said to him, 'Father, I have sinned against heaven and against you, I am no longer worthy to be called your son.'
- Luke 15:21

Prayer

Jesus, I know you are my one true advocate. You are always present and always working. I trust that you are in the arena, ready to fight with me as I battle this lie. Come, shatter the stronghold of rebellion in me.

Thoughts we ponder...

AS A FOLLOWER OF CHRIST, HOW DO YOU APPROACH THE THRONE OF GRACE DURING A TIME OF REBELLION?

In Luke 15, we hear a story of the prodigal son that rebelled against his Father. The son left the father and spent all his inheritance. He eventually returned home to the father to find work and a way to eat. When we hear this story, our focus is often on the prodigal son. However, the story is equally about the Father and his heart for his son. His love never changed, and the moment he saw the son coming home, he ran to him. While our rebellion doesn't shock God, and he loves us in our humanness, it does hurt the Father as He watches the pain our rebellion causes us.

Let's Take This To Jesus ~

Jesus, your heart begs of me, that while I may struggle and stray, to not let my season of rebellion turn into multiple seasons or even a lifetime. I trust that You love me in my rebellion, in my humanness. Your word says that our battle is not against flesh and blood (one another), but the enemy himself. I know how the enemy wants to keep me from understanding this truth. Help me to believe that your heart is for me. I pray that my heart would not run away from you. Help me learn how to remain close and talk to you while battling my strongholds. Please continue speaking to my heart that your desire is for me to turn back to you. You want me to come home.

REFLECTIONS FROM THE HEART

When looking at this stronghold...

What is Jesus revealing to you?

Does this perspective differ from what
you thought before? If so, how?

What new thoughts are you having?

How can His unconditional love encourage you?

Luke 15:21

Luke 15:21

MY INTENTION

AWARENESS

What have I become aware of in this chapter?
What is something new I've learned?

BELIEF

What were my thoughts around this stronghold
before and after? Did I uncover any lies?

COMMITMENT

What truth will I move forward believing? Is there
something I want to stay committed to working on?

Intentions

Luke 15:21

Luke 15:21

His Banner Over Me is Love

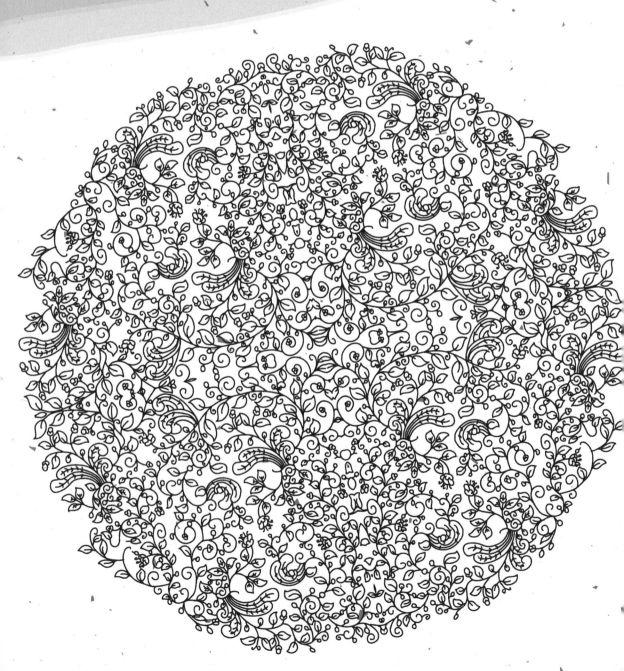

Reflection

Shatter the Stronghold of

Fear

My peace I leave with you;
my peace I give you.
I do not give it as the world gives.
- John 14:27

Prayer

Jesus, I know you are my one true advocate. You are always present and always working. I trust that you are in the arena, ready to fight with me as I battle this lie. Come, shatter the stronghold of fear in me.

Thoughts we ponder...

AS A HUMAN BEING, WE FACE FEAR EVERY DAY. IT IS A VERY REAL PART OF OUR LIVES. JESUS HAD EVERY REASON TO REACT TO FEAR AS WE OFTEN DO. WHY DO YOU THINK HE DIDN'T?

When you know all that Jesus endured and went through, you know that he had every reason to be afraid. It could be easy for us to say that he wasn't because he was Jesus, that He knew all things, and He knew the Father. However, what Jesus modeled for us was choosing to trust--in the midst of what we do not understand. Releasing fear and choosing to trust does not mean you know the outcome of a situation; it means you TRUST the one who does. Your negative circumstances may not change, but Jesus offers peace in the midst of whatever you are facing. Lean in and ask Jesus how you can open your hand to trust him a little more; await the peace that will be added to your life.

Let's Take This To Jesus ~

Jesus, help me see that the biggest thing that has to change when I feel fear is me. I have to change how I process fear and my beliefs surrounding my control of circumstances or the outcome. Remind me, Lord, that I must choose to exercise the muscle of courage. Empower me to tap into the Holy Spirit that lives within me. I want the fruit of peace to be evident in my heart and life. Please help me to intentionally seek the path that brings your peace.

REFLECTIONS FROM THE HEART

When looking at this stronghold...

What is Jesus revealing to you?

Does this perspective differ from what
you thought before? If so, how?

What new thoughts are you having?

How can His unconditional love encourage you?

John 14:27

John 14:27

MY INTENTION

AWARENESS

What have I become aware of in this chapter?
What is something new I've learned?

BELIEF

What were my thoughts around this stronghold
before and after? Did I uncover any lies?

COMMITMENT

What truth will I move forward believing? Is there
something I want to stay committed to working on?

Intentions

John 14:27

John 14:27

His Banner Over Me is Love

Reflection

Shatter the Stronghold of

Bitterness

See to it that no ones falls short of the grace of God and that no bitter root grows up to cause trouble...
- Hebrews 12:15

Prayer

Jesus, I know you are my one true advocate. You are always present and always working. I trust that you are in the arena, ready to fight with me as I battle this lie. Come, shatter the stronghold of bitterness in me.

Thoughts we ponder...

JESUS HAD EVERY REASON TO BE BITTER. WHAT DO YOU THINK HELPED HIM EMBODY KINDNESS TOWARDS HUMANITY INSTEAD?

Bitterness can be a byproduct of unforgiveness and the inability to process ongoing hurt or pain. One doesn't usually become "bitter" at the person that cut you off on the highway. In that case, it's probably frustration or anger that you are feeling. It's when something is ongoing that one may find themselves becoming bitter. The best antidote that we have found to cure bitterness is to embody Jesus's words in Luke 23:34, "Father forgive them for they know not what they do." Living this out requires not taking others' words and actions personally, choosing not to take offense. Ask God to change your heart so that it truly releases and forgives people, always but especially when they don't understand what they've done or the impact of their choices.

Let's Take This To Jesus ~

Jesus, I ask that you clear away all bitterness in me. Encourage me to always come to you with my broken heart. You have every right to be bitter towards me, but you choose to show me grace. Give me your spirit to be a vessel of your love and your ways unto others just as you are to me. Jesus, please remind me of the power within me to be like you in offering kindness to others even when they don't deserve it. I am shaped by you the most as I see you showing me kindness I do not deserve. May this spur me on to love more as you do.

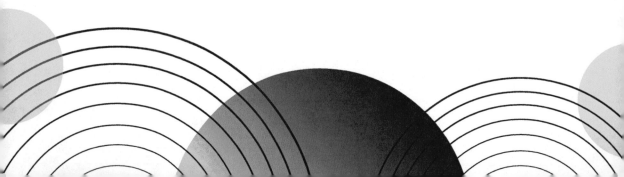

REFLECTIONS FROM THE HEART

When looking at this stronghold...

What is Jesus revealing to you?

Does this perspective differ from what you thought before? If so, how?

What new thoughts are you having?

How can His unconditional love encourage you?

Hebrews 12:15

Hebrews 12:15

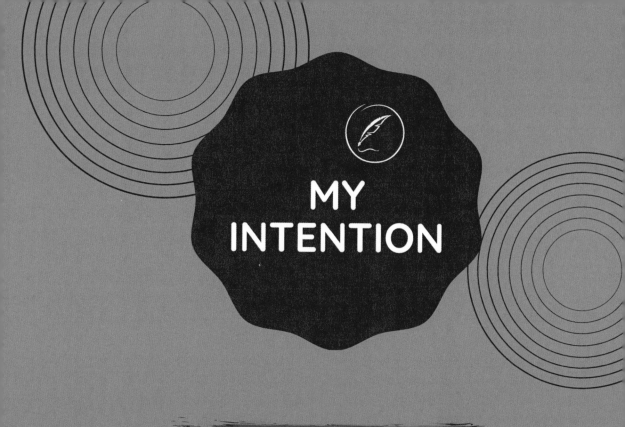

MY INTENTION

AWARENESS

What have I become aware of in this chapter?
What is something new I've learned?

BELIEF

What were my thoughts around this stronghold
before and after? Did I uncover any lies?

COMMITMENT

What truth will I move forward believing? Is there
something I want to stay committed to working on?

Intentions

Hebrews 12:15

Hebrews 12:15

His Banner Over Me is Love

Reflection

FOR MORE RESOURCES

ONLINE ACCESS

COMING SOON!

SHATTER THE STRONGHOLDS ~ GUIDED PRAYER BOOK & JOURNAL

SHATTER THE STRONGHOLDS

PRAYER BOOK & Journal

"Take heart. Lean into the positive, stronghold truths that God says over you. This book contains 10 strongholds. Know that moving through even a single stronghold is taking a huge step closer to being free."

– Amber Lynn

FIND FREEDOM. BREAK OFF STRONGHOLDS.

FREE ADDITIONAL WORKSHEETS

WWW.JENNIFERTRACY-INSPIRE.COM/BOOKS

MEET
AMBER

Amber Lynn is a Colorado native who is tethered by Jesus and her community. Since 2010 she has shared her powerful story through her speaking and writing endeavors. Her passion is to see life change happen through vulnerable, authentic connections. She wants her hands and heart to be a part of that. Whether it's speaking to a crowd of thousands or one on one, she's in!

Amber is known for infusing JOY into every person and situation she encounters. Her joy is like glitter! Creating is one of her greatest gifts - painting, songwriting, or anything in between! Art is an outlet that she has used all of her life to process grief and triumph, to express both her song of praise and sorrow. A great day involves using both the left and right sides of her brain.

She is immensely grateful for the quality time she gets to spend with her sweet sister McKayla and the wonderful friends God has put in her life. Her family has played an enormous role in shaping who she is today.

MEET JENNIFER

Jennifer Tracy was born and raised in Colorado and resided there until 2018. She has deep roots in Northern Colorado, with many friends and family still living there, including her two exquisitely beautiful adult daughters, McKayla and Amber.

Jennifers courageous move to Florida though bittersweet brought the ocean's tranquility and freedom from the permanent pain she faced after her Chiari I Brain Malformation Decompression in 2012. The move to Florida led to many new beginnings, including business endeavors, a song collaboration with her daughter Amber, and meeting the love of her life, Jeremy Fleeman, in late 2018. Jennifer and Jeremy recently married and reside in Tallahassee. They share a love of music, travel, road trips, spontaneous karaoke, and cooking together.

Jennifer finds deep strength and inspiration from her faith, family, and her friends. Now that her daughters are grown, she finds herself being a bit more adventurous. She lives out her most significant purpose in two distinct ways- enjoying life on this side of grief with her daughters and family and through her business endeavors as a life coach, National Speaker, and writer. One of her all-time favorite books is Wild at Heart by John Eldredge.

 WWW.JENNIFERTRACY-INSPIRE.COM

Made in the USA
Middletown, DE
07 May 2023

30167991R00084